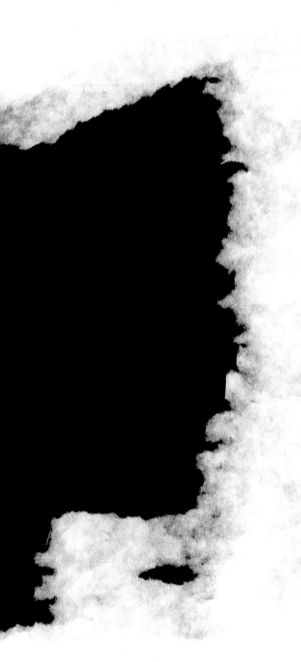

Let's Visit France

Susie Brooks

PowerKiDS
press™

New York

Published in 2010 by The Rosen Publishing Group Inc.
29 East 21st Street, New York, NY 10010

First Edition

Library of Congress Cataloging-in-Publication Data

Brooks, Susie.
  Let's visit France / Susie Brooks.
    p. cm. -- (Around the world)
  Includes index.
  ISBN 978-1-4358-3026-4 (library binding)
  ISBN 978-1-4358-8606-3 (paperback)
  ISBN 978-1-4358-8607-0 (6-pack)
  1. France--Description and travel--Juvenile literature.
  2. France--Juvenile literature. I. Title.
  DC29.3.B76 2010
  914.404'84--dc22

                    2008051880

Manufactured in China

Note to parents and teachers
The projects and activities in this book
are designed to be completed by children.
However, we recommend adult supervision
at all times since the Publisher cannot be
held responsible for any injury caused
while completing the projects.

Web Sites
Due to the changing nature of Internet
links, PowerKids Press has developed
an online list of Web sites related to
the subject of this book. This site
is updated regularly. Please use this
link to access this list:
www.powerkidslinks.com/world/france

Picture Credits
p5: © qaphotos.com/Alamy; p6: © Roy Rainford/Robert Harding World Imagery/Corbis; p7: © David Spurdens/
Corbis; p8: © Lourens Smak/Alamy; p9: © Bruno Barbier/Robert Harding World Imagery/Corbis; p10: © G. Bowater/
Corbis; p11: © Wayland Picture Library; p12: © Free Agents Limited/Corbis; p13: © Paul Almasy/Corbis; © Owen
Franken/Corbis; © Wayland; © Katie Powell; p14: © AFP/Getty Images; p15: © Durand Patrick/Corbis Sygma; p16:
© Ted Spiegel/Corbis; p17: Geoffrey Clements/Corbis; p18: © Owen Franken/Corbis; p19 © Tom Brakefield/Corbis;
p20: © James Quigley/Getty; p21: © Wayland Picture Library; p22: © Chev Wilkinson/Getty; p23: © AFP/Getty
Images; ©; p24: © Bernard Annebicque/Corbis Sygma; p25: © Getty Images; p26, title page: © Schlegelmilch/
Corbis; p27: ©; ©; p28: © Reuters/Corbis; p29: © Jeff Vespa/Contributor/Getty.

Cover: Eiffel Tower © Free Agents Limited/Corbis; Snowboarder near Mont Blanc © David Spurdens/Corbis.

Contents

This is France!

France is a big country in western Europe. Many people who come here on vacation fly to Paris, the capital city.

This map shows just a few of the many places to visit in France.

UNITED KINGDOM

BELGIUM

GERMANY

Giverny

Paris

Strasbourg

Le Mans

F R A N C E

La Rochelle

Provence

ITALY

Nimes

Lourdes

Cannes

Pyrénées mountains

S P A I N

From the U.K., you can take a train through the Channel Tunnel under the sea! There are ferries that go to France, too.

On a Channel Tunnel train, you can't tell you are deep under water!

It was exciting arriving in France, but I couldn't understand what people were saying!

Speak French!

hello
bonjour (bon-j**hor**)

thank you
merci (mair-**see**)

please
s'il vous plait (see-voo-p**lai**)

Sunshine and snow

France is a good place to visit for warm summer weather. Lots of people head for the sunny beaches in the south of the country.

River swimming under the Pont du Gard bridge is fun on a hot summer's day.

Speak French!

sun
soleil (sol-**ay**)

snow
niege (nee-**ehj**)

beach
plage (**plahj**e)

6

Winter brings people to the mountains for skiing and other snow sports. It is cold on the slopes, but the sun is still very strong.

This snowboarder is in the Alps, near France's highest mountain, Mont Blanc.

I put on so much sunscreen, my nose was white—it looked funny but I didn't get burned.

Somewhere to sleep

France is famous for its **chateaux**, like this one in the Loire Valley.

People who visit French cities and seaside towns usually stay in hotels or **apartments**. In the countryside, your bed could be in a cottage—or a castle!

Houseboats are popular in France—there are beds inside.

Some people rent vacation homes called gites. In the mountains, you might stay in a **chalet**. Camping is fun if you like adventure and the weather is good.

Speak French!

bedroom
chambre (shom-bre)

bathroom
salle de bain (sal-de-ban)

shower
douche (doosh)

Speeding around

France has some of the fastest trains in the world. Traveling from city to city by train is usually much quicker than going by car.

TGV trains speed along at up to 186 miles (300 km) per hour!

There are plenty of free cycle paths in France. This one is near a river.

If you want to enjoy the scenery in France, go on a bike ride. Cycle along a river—there will be lots to see and hopefully, not many hills!

On French roads

- People drive on the right-hand side of the road, just like at home.
- You can't travel in the front of a car until you are 10.
- Drivers have to pay to use most highways.

11

Action-packed Paris

This is the Eiffel Tower. You can take an elevator all the way up to the top.

No one gets bored in Paris! France's capital city is famous for its art, fashion, and impressive buildings.

While you're here...

Pick your favorite picture inside the Louvre...

and the Pompidou Center art galleries.

Play or watch a puppet show in one of the city parks.

Spot the funny **gargoyles** on Notre Dame Cathedral.

Take a ride on...

- a **carousel** in the Tuileries gardens
- a boat along the River Seine
- an underground **Metro** train—count the stops!

13

Great day trips

Don't miss these places just outside Paris.

Meet the characters at Parc Asterix before you go on all the rides.

Park Asterix

A fun park based on France's favorite comic book hero, Asterix, and his friend, Obelix.

We spent a day at Euro Disney—
I wanted to go on all the rides,
but there wasn't enough time!

Palace of Versailles

Look for:

- The Hall of Mirrors
- The Neptune and Dragon fountains
- Rowboats and a mini-train.

France Miniature

Visit France Miniature to see famous places, toy-sized! Paris's Arc de Triomphe looks tiny here.

Speak French!

garden
jardin (jhar-da)

ticket
billet (bee-yay)

park
parc (park)

15

Northern sights

Go to see the Bayeux tapestry. It's like a giant comic strip!

A little farther away from Paris, but within easy reach, are more popular sights. Every year, thousands of people visit Mont St. Michel—a magical abbey on a rock in the sea.

A trip to Giverny shows you France through an artist's eyes. This was the home of Monet, one of the country's best-known painters.

Look for Monet's bridge and water lilies in the garden at Giverny.

Paint like Monet!

- Use blobs of bright colors.
- Paint flowers, fields, or the seaside.
- Paint in different weathers.

Traveling south

Many people go on driving vacations through France. Traveling south from Paris, here are some things you might see.

Thick forests full of wildlife →

People picking grapes to make wine

Fields full of bright yellow sunflowers →

Wild, white horses in the marshy **Camargue**

 Castles and bridges made of sand-colored stone

 The Pyrenees Mountains

The great aquarium at La Rochelle, on the west coast

Purple fields of lavender

The Mediterranean Sea

Tasty treats

In France, you will always find good things to eat. There is a huge choice of cheeses, meats, fruits, cakes, and pastries.

Take a picnic to the park, with a basket of bread, pâté, grapes, and salami.

Dad's favorite food was snails—yuck! They were really chewy and tasted like garlic!

Eating in cafés is popular in French cities. You can often sit outside. French bread is served with every meal.

Don't forget to try a thin pancake, called a crêpe, in France.

On the menu

baguette (bag-**ett**)
a stick of bread

fromage (from-**ah**-je)
cheese

boisson (bwa-son)
drink

21

Time to shop

France has some gigantic supermarkets, but it can be more fun to buy your food in an open-air market or small local shop.

Patisseries such as this one have mouth-watering displays.

The money people spend in France is called the euro.

The city of Strasbourg has a popular market at Christmas time.

French cities are famous for their small, chic shops called boutiques. Look for **souvenirs** to take home, such as lace from **Normandy** or pottery from **Provence**.

Speak French!

bakery
boulangerie (boo-**lon**-jair-ee)

cake shop
patisserie (pat-**ee**-sair-ee)

newspaper shop
tabac (tab-ack)

Being French

When you visit France, you'll learn a little about how the French people live. You might notice different traditions around the country.

In the boggy Landes region, shepherds used to walk on stilts like these local dancers.

There are many different religions in France. **Roman Catholics** are the biggest group. They worship in beautiful churches and cathedrals.

Millions of Roman Catholics visit the holy town of Lourdes every year, to pray or help people in need.

When I met my French cousins, they kissed me on both cheeks!

Speak French!

mother
mère (maire)

father
père (paire)

sister
sœur (sur)

brother
frère (fraire)

25

Ready to play

Many people visit France to see big sports events. The Tour de France is a huge cycling race. At Le Mans and Monaco, there is famous car racing.

The Monaco Grand Prix is a daring race around twisty streets!

Other popular sports include soccer, rugby, and **boules**. On the coasts, you can swim, windsurf, and even sail yachts across the sand.

With boules, you have to roll your ball as close to the little marker ball as you can.

At the Tour de France, people write the names of their favorite cyclists on the road.

Festival fever

Being in France on July 14 means being at a party! This is **Bastille Day**, France's biggest festival. Watch for fireworks, flags, and loud marching bands.

A famous Bastille Day parade marches through the Arc de Triomphe in Paris.

Many regions have their own festivals. The city of Cannes hosts a huge film festival every year, when movie stars come from all over the world.

A big red carpet is laid out for the stars at Cannes. Not many people are lucky enough to go!

Party places

Lemon festival Menton (February/March) see giant lemon sculptures and fruity floats!		Wind festival Calvi, Corsica (October/ November) fly kites, watch windmills, and more!	

Make it yourself

France has a crêpe for everyone. Make these and find your favorite flavor!

You will need:

- pre-prepared crêpes
- aluminum foil or baking parchment
- a selection of toppings (see right).

Crêpes

1. Ask an adult to cook or heat up the crêpes. Stack them with pieces of aluminum foil or baking parchment between them so they don't stick together.

2. Experiment with different yummy toppings! Try the ideas on the opposite page.

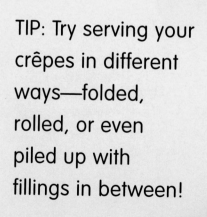

Sweet
- Melted chocolate chips and banana
- Lemon juice with sugar or sprinkles
- Strawberry preserves and vanilla ice cream

Savory
- Cheese and ham (heat this up again to melt the cheese)
- Cream cheese and chopped tomatoes
- Ratatouille (a cooked vegetable mix)

TIP: Try serving your crêpes in different ways—folded, rolled, or even piled up with fillings in between!

Useful words and further information

apartment	A room or rooms for living in.
Bastille Day	A national holiday celebrating an important battle of 1789.
boules	A game where people roll metal balls along the ground.
Camargue	A marshy plain in the south of France.
carousel	A merry-go-round.
chalet	A type of wooden house, common in the Alps.
chateau (plural chateaux)	A French castle.
gargoyle	A waterspout carved in the shape of a strange figure.
Metro	The underground train system in Paris.
Normandy	A region in northwest France.
Provence	A region in southeast France.
Roman Catholic	A type of Christian.
souvenir	Something you take home to remind you of somewhere you have been.

Books to read

Bonjour L'Enfant!: A Child's Tour of France by Danna Troncatty Leahy (Authorhouse, 2006)

Countries of the World: France by Michael Dahl (Capstone Press, 1999)

Country Explorers: France by Tom Streissguth (Lerner Publications, 2008)

France ABCs: A Book About the People and Places of France by Katz Cooper (Picture Window Books, 2003)

Living in France by Ruth Thomson (Sea to Sea Publications, 2007)